ARCHAEOLOGICAL MUSEUM
FLORENCE

Text by: FRANCESCO RAZETO
for the grek - Etruscan - Roman Collections

Text by: MARINO MARINI
for the Egyptian Collection

Becocci Editore Florence

© 1985 Editrice GIUSTI di Becocci-Firenze
Printing: Kina Italia S.p.A. – Milano
Photographs: Ovidio Guaita, Becocci Archives,
Kina Italia Archives, Florence Tourist Agency,
I.F.I. – Firenze, Scala - Firenze
Impagination: Renzo Matino – Schio

FIRENZE AND THE ARCHAEOLOGICAL MUSEUM

FRANCESCO RAZETO

In a city like Florence which has always been considered daughter and heiress to Rome, the love for classical antiquity has always thrived, reaching the point of forming an actual cult with the Neoplatonic Academy of Lorenzo il Magnifico (of the Medici) and his court of men of letters. But already with his grandfather Cosimo the Elder the palace in via Larga, today via Cavour, became the mecca for the artistic and literary life of the period, and Florence the motivating center of a new culture no longer exclusively latin as in the medieval period. Thus a cultural unity of the classical world was recomposed – born in Greece and assimilated in Rome – thanks also to the fundamental contribution of the wise greek sages of the court of Constantinople who were guests in the palace of via Larga on the occasion of the Ecumenical Council of 1439. Together with texts in the original language of Plato, the "too much house for so small a family", as Cosimo the Elder had said, was enriched with works of art from antiquity: like the snorting head of a horse, adapted in a garden fountain and which inspired Donatello for his monument of Gattamelata, various sarcophaghi in the Uffizi which gave inspiration to the young Michelangelo for his Battle of the Centaurs (at the Casa Buonarroti), and the sarcophagus with the Triumph of Dionysus, with a playful bacchante, not by chance at the feet of the Primavera of Botticelli. Lorenzo il Magnifico, patron of antiquities, collected precious 'objects': inlaid hard (semiprecious) stones, cameos and cut/engraved glass which were then reproduced and enlarged in medallions in the courtyard of the palace; roman and oriental vases mounted by goldsmiths where one sees the balls of the coat-of-arms and the ring with the diamond star, Medici symbols intertwined (Museum of Silver in Palazzo Pitti).

Following the aesthetic taste, refined but heterogeneous, of il Magnifico, comes the political interest of Cosimo I. His official title is Dux Florentiae from 1537, then Magnus Dux (Grand duke) Etruriae from 1569, as his duke-dom occupies more or less the territory of Etruria, a region of the Roman Empire. His family of rich bankers is therefore ennobled in his research of his illustrious ancestors. His love for 'etruscanisms' – that only now is beginning to be classified within the generic classical arts – was fruit of political calculations, an historical justification of the recently acquired power over a region already unified in ancient times. The discovery and restoration of certain masterpieces of the Archaeological Museum (often with fantasy but entrusted to great artists) took place in the period of his grand duke-dom e.g. the Arringatore, the Chimera and the Minerva of Arezzo as well as various bronzes.

With his successors the Medici collections are further enriched: Vittoria della Rovere, in 1633, brought with her as part of her dowry to husband Ferdinand II, the famous "Idolino" with a magnificent renaissance base (together with the principal group of works by Raphael which are today in the Pitti Palace).

With the end of the Medici line, in 1743, there begins the advent of the House of Lorraine. These were obliged by the 'Family Pact' of the last grand duchess Maria Luisa Medici to never disperse the artistic collections, but to conserve them instead as an inalienable patrimony of the florentine

3

people. The Medici collections of antiquities were then reunited in the Uffizi. A guide book of the last century (Fantozzi, 1844) tells us that in the 'West Corridor' of the Uffizi are found the 'collection of bronzes' including the above-mentioned statues, the collection of antique vases, that of inscriptions, of gems and hard stones, "in all, 14 large cabinets plus other smaller ones", as well as even 39 etruscan sarcophaghi.

With the creation of the Italian Kingdom, the heterogeneous collections of the Uffizi found a new location (1871) in various specialized museums: the etruscan collection was placed – together with the egyptian to which a separate chapter is dedicated – in the Cenacolo di Foligno in via Faenza. It was then transfered in 1880 to the actual location, the palace 'della Crocetta'

constructed in the 17th century by Giulio Parigi for the grand duchess Maria Maddalena of Austria.

In 1898 the Topographical Museum of Etruria was inaugurated, requested by the director of the museum, Luigi Adriano Milani. Before the flood of 1966 which devastated the long ground floor corridor constituting the Topographical Museum, the entrance was situated in via Gino Capponi. This part of the museum – where finds from various locations of Etruria are joined together in room after room providing a picture of the local artistic production – is still waiting to be restructured definitively (Feb. 1985). The entrance hall of that time has since been redesigned and has recently housed the Bronzes of Riace, the Frontone of Talamone and a documentary exhibition on the excavations of Pompei.

Horse's head from an equestrian monument from the Hellenistic period. Once in the garden of Palazzo Medici where it was adapted as part of a fountain.

Etruria

According to the administrative division of Augustus in imperial roman times, the name "Etruria" designated the VIIth region which was bathed to the west by the Tyrrhenian Sea and having as natural boarders to the north the Magra River and the Apennines Mountains, to the south and west the Tiber River for its entire course.

The territory with traces of settlements of the Etruscans (or 'Tuyrsenoi' for the Greeks, 'Etruschi' or 'Tusci' for the Latins, 'Rasenna' as they called themselves) was originally much larger and comprised vast areas beyond these limits: etruscan finds were discovered in Campania (the Capua tile) and in the valley of the Po River (the Piacenza liver) where undoubtably there were etruscan cities. For example: Marzabotto (the etruscan 'Misa'), the ports of Spina and Adria at the ancient mouth of the Po River, Mantova protected by the lakes of the Mincio River, Felsina (today Bologna) whose 'suburb' Villanova gave its name to a particular cultural *facies* (type) of the 9th-7th centuries B.C.

The most highly populated zone was the Maremma which was also the first to decline because it turned to swamp and malaria set in (and it was known as "Maritima hora", between the Cecina and Tiber Rivers). The cities were often settled far from the coast but with access to the sea, or else castled on the tufaceous plateaus (Tarquinia, Cerveteri and, inland, Orvieto); or protected by the bend of a river (Vulci, Veio). The position of Populonia was singular: directly on the seacoast, it was a docking point and a place where iron from Elba Island and the 'Metal Hills' (Colline Metallifere) was worked.

The Question of Origin

The problem of the origin of the Etruscans was born in antiquity from the discordance of classical sources. Herodotus (Vth cent. B.C.) and Strabo spoke of a famine that forced half the population of Lydia, under the guidance of Tirrhenos, son of King Athis, to search for new land – already inhabited by the Umbrians -- with a possible link to the coast of the sea which is in fact named after him: the

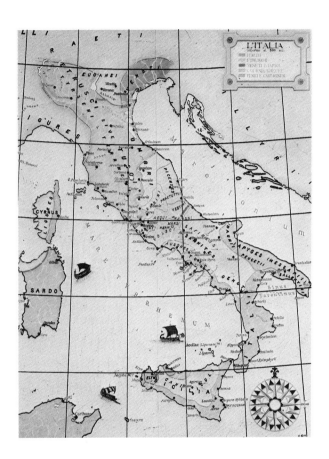

Tyrrhenian Sea. Ellanico of Mitilene (Vth cent. B.C.) identifies them as the Pelasgians, a mythical people, navigators, who penetrated the delta of the Po River. Still another theory (Anticlide, according to Strabo) speaks of the Pelasgians' arrival with the first coming of the Tirreni; Dionysius of Halicarnassus (Ist cent. B.C.) maintains that the Etruscans themselves claimed to be indigenous – in contrast to the other theories – and thus arises the ancient question. Latin authors (Servius in the comments of the Aeneid, Livy in the 5th book of the Histories) augment the Etruscan presence from the Alps to Sicily. It was exactly this peremptory interpretation in a passage of the Histories (V, 33) where it speaks of an alpine people, in particular the "Reti", as of etruscan origin, which gave birth to a third hypothesis – besides the eastern origin and the indigenous one – origin from the north.

Although establishing legitimate similarities between the Etruscan civilisation and the eastern world, today archaeological research is incline to leave off the question of origin so important as to absorb all attention as in the past. A civilisation that is so rich and complex, such a fundamental part of every cultural contribution in the Mediterranean area, can not be born from a simple operation, transplant or colonization, but is formed instead, through contact with other peoples of the Mediterranean in the course of seven centuries.

That which interests us today is the development of their civilisation, that which they assimilated from other cultures and that which they passed on. The problem of the origin as fascinating as it is, though fruitless, should not deter us from a thorough study of the characteristics of their culture so diversified in space and time.

The Problem of the Language

Today we read Etruscan without difficulty. The alphabet is Greek chaldean, which arrived in Italy through Cumae and Pithecusa (the contemporary Ischia), colony of Calcide, city of Eubea: the long island off the coast (east) of Attica. The uncertainties regarding the phonetic value of certain signs have been resolved (and which had been protracted since the end of the 1400's from the time when Annio from Viterbo presented the problem). Usually it is read from right to left but the contrary also exists as in archaic Greek. In this text it is transcribed in the Latin alphabet as well as are the inscriptions in Greek. The problem is therefore not how to read Etruscan-'decipher' according to a common and trite idea that tenaciously resists – but how to interpret it, to understand it. And here arise the problems: the documents in our possession are many, about 15,000, but for the most part they deal with proper names, funerary inscriptions according to a standard model (names and offices held, parental relationships, age, somentimes a brief eulogy of the deceased) and brief dedicatory formulae.

Traces remain with the latin authors of an etruscan literature which was certainly absorbed, elaborated and adapted to the literature of Rome: regarding the texts, above all, of the prophetic or divinitory art of which the Etruscans were absolute masters. For example, the *libri augurales* on the interpretation of the flight of birds, *libri fulgurales* on lightning, *libri haruspicini* on the observation of the vital organs of animals, *libri rituales* on the foundation of cities. It is probably even still a continuation in language, in the sacerdotal environment, until the Empire. The 19th century philologists were anxious in the quest for a relationship between Etruscan and other known languages, coming to the conclusion that Etruscan is not a Indo-European language, a conviction that continues today. Of the great quantity of literature on the subject we refer to a text that makes a point of the situation: R.A. Staccioli, *Il Mistero della lingua etrusca* ('The mystery of the etruscan language') Roma, 1977. The latest contribution, received with comprehensible skepticism in the academic environment, is Piero Bernardini Marzolla, *L'etrusco, una lingua ritrovata* ('Etruscan, a rediscovered language'), Mondadori, October 1984. It is a convincing and impassioned text where one does not grope about comparing singular etruscan words with those of one or another ancient language creating a chaotic language or "babel". It instead nears itself – based on a system of precise corresponding phonetics – to a singular language, sanskrit, the ancient indian language completely documented, enriched during the course of a migration from a country strongly indianized off the coast of Asia Minor. There remain some 'dark spots' or doubts, but still today it is impossible to find a more organic, clearer and nearly indisputable treatise. From this moment, then, we encourage you to read this, besides which it is very smooth going, convinced that we will hear it being spoken about; also because in this way the problem of the origins would obviously be resolved.

The François Vase

An entire room of the ground floor is dedicated to one of the most famous masterpieces of greek vase painting; it was found in the metropolis of Fonte Rotella near Chiusi. The room also presents in the panels on the walls the eventful vicissitudes of the discovery of the vase and numerous restorations.

It is an archaic Attica 'krater' (italian 'cratere', large vase with wide mouth) with volutes datable according to the style (black and red figures on a natural background, in perspective on an ionic profile) at 570 B.C. It is unique in its accuracy of pictorial techniques, the vivacity and the variety of the scenes. Each figure (there have been counted about 250) is rendered with the most minute detail – and is accompanied by his proper name – as well as some of the buildings. The speed of the horses is shown by doubling some of the profiles.

It presents itself as an imposing object of quality; of unusually large dimensions, it is to be 'read' as a text of celebrative mythology complete with protagonists and personalities as border. It was not destined – as was the common use – to be an urn from which aromatic and watered wine was drawn during banquets.

On the handles, Gorgons with a "Lady of the fair" or the persian Artemis and Ajax who carries the cadaver of Achilles.

From top to bottom, Side A – Border: the wild boar hunt of Calidone who has already knocked down a dog and a hunter and is attacked from behind by pursuers armed with lances, while two other figures try to grasp its snout to pierce it; also with, on the sides, archers – some in the scita costume – ready to shoot arrows.

– Chariot race in honor of Patroclus, pieces missing; on the left, under the horses, the tripod, customary gift for the winner.

– This is the only scene that develops around the vase without interuption even with the double attachment of the handles. On the right, Thetis, of whom we catch a glimpse through the halfway open door of the house/temple; and Peleus, standing, who with Thetis receive the gift of the court of the gods of Olympus, introduced by the centaur Chiron. In front of him, vertically, one reads from top to bottom, "Clizia designed me" (the vase is speaking);

Theseus and Dionysus with an amphora are following, two seasons, (still another signature, that of the potter: "Ergotimo made me"), Calliope, Zeus on a chariot accompanied by Hera and surrounded by muses.

In between the handles, where they are attached to the vase, the wagon of Amphitrite; then proceeding in the same direction, Aphrodite, Ares, Athena, the Moire of good fortune for weddings, Maia, Hermes and Kronos (Time) – after the gap.

– The ambush of Achilles to Troilus: a prophesy claimed that Troy would not have fallen if Troilus, the youngest of fifty sons of Priam, would have reached his 20th year. Troilus who went out to draw water from a source, on the left where there is still a trojan protected by Apollo, let the amphora fall and flees, galloping towards the walls of Troy, chased by Achilles (missing) who is assisted by Hera and Athena: the old father anxiously awaits him outside the gate, from which come out some warriors to rescue.

– The frieze with palmettes (stylized palm leaf), sphinxes, and animal combat, the simple decoration of stylized rays, and, in the fort, a battle between pygmies and cranes, continuing on the two sides of the krater.

Side B – Border: on the left the landing of Theseus (a companion dove in to swim in his enthusiasm) and the return of the 14 youths and young ladies who are holding hands, alternating, in the act of dancing, and who are destined to be sacrificed to the Minotaur.

– Scene of centauromachia: struggle of the centaurs against the Lapiths, with the episode of the giant Kaineus.

– Return of Hephaestus, preceeded by Dionysus and accompanied by silenus, to Olympus where Aphrodite awaits him, who will be his bride, terrified by his ugliness, Zeus and Hera enthroned, Athena, Artemis and Ares.

The vase exalts the enterprises of the two Attica heroes, par excellence, Achilles and Theseus; Achilles' affection for his companion Patroclus and his divine extraction.

Because of the central band with the bridal procession, the supposition has been made that we are dealing with a wedding gift that the deceased wanted to take with him to his tomb.

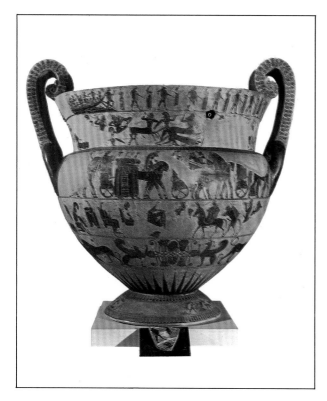

Room of the Cinerary Urns from Chiusi (Clusium)

The three cinerary urns on display represent the 'point of arrival' in the evolution of the archaic Canopic vase, an ovoidal cinerary vase with human head and a hint of arms. Under the influence of Greek classic art, in the Vth ventury B.C., the entire body of the defunct was represented with a variety of poses and a powerful plasticity: here the tendency of abstraction, typical of Chiusi art, reaches a sober monumentality and effects of composure and solemnity. Originally in polychrome, the urns in "fetid stone" hide in their interior a cavity for the ashes and for which the head functions as lid.

To the left of the entrance, on the lid of a missing coffin, a 'lasa' with a scroll in its hand containing originally a funerary eulogy. It surprises the unaware defunct reclining 'banquet style' and it extends its wing to snatch him.

In the following one, complete, a couple: the husband, leaning on a *Kline*, holds with his left hand an umbilicated patera (container used in sacrifices to hold the blood of the victim or else for libation) and rests his right hand on the shoulder of his consort who is sitting and who turns to look at him pulling her veil aside (it is probable that the couple looked each other in the eye). Next to this, a non-pertinent head, readapted in a 19th century 'restoration' which was often conducted with no scientific

criteria.

The urn on the right where the integrations have been made evident, usually glazed accurately to give the impression of authenticity, is the "*Mater Matuta*" (goddess of the morning and of the sunrise, ancient italic divinity eventually confused with the greek Leucothea). It is the epithet commonly attributed to this urn representing a mother with her son in her lap sitting on a cube-shaped throne flanked by sphinxes, squatting as if the armrests. The artist wanted to represent with her the hieratic and solemn pose, not motherly affection; but also with the sacral quality of the figure in a kind of 'heroine-izing' of the deceased.

The Christian theme of the Madonna with Child finds here its remote progenitor: Arnolfo di Cambio and Giotto could have been familiar with similar statues.

In the cabinet next to it, together with fragments of the 19th century restoration, the elegant Attica *oinochoe*, trilobed, in the form of a female head. And there is the large gold brooch with the catch in the form of three pomegranates set in a triangle, executed with a mixed technique, dust and granulation. They were objects dear to the deceased and proof of his high rank, part of his funerary furnishings.

The Milani Room

This room is dedicated to L.A. Milani who was asked in 1879 to reorganize the etruscan section of the florentine antiquarium and was the founder of the Topographical Museum. Here are displayed three works of art which are thus entitled:

the "Apollo", bought by Milani together with the "Apollino" from the abbot Ubaldo Bellini of Osimo (Ancona), belonging to his family from the 1700's.

The denomination "Apollo" is improper: it is a greek *Kouros* (the corresponding female is a *Kore*) in Parian marble. One of the principal themes of archaic statuary, it was the representation of the ideal male beauty, a synthesis of force and harmony, and stripped of all contingent elements; it was an expression of a serene vitality and a secure domination over nature. And it was not necessarily an image of a divine cult, but instead, according to

The François Vase: Side A From top to bottom: The Wild boar Hunt of Calidone, Chariot Race in honor of Patroclus, Procession for the marriage of Peleus and Thetis, The Attack of Achilles on Troilus

VASO DETTO FRANÇOIS PERCHÈ RINVENUTO DA FRANCESCO FRANÇOIS NEL 1844 A FONTE DI ROTELLA PRESSO CHIUSI. CAPO-LAVORO DELLA CERAMICA ARCAICA. FIRMATO DAL VASAIO ERGO-TIMOS E DAL PITTORE KLEITIAS.
NELLE SEI ZONE DI DECORAZIONE SONO TRATTATI I SEGUENTI SOGGETTI: 1° CACCIA AL CINGHIALE CALIDONIO E DANZA DI TESEO DI ARIANNA E DEI LORO COMPAGNI; 2° GIUOCHI FUNEBRI IN ONORE DI PATROCLO, E LOTTA DEI CENTAURI E DEI LAPITI; 3° NOZZE DI PELEO E DI TETIDE; 4°AGGUATO DI ACHILLE A TROILO, E RITORNO DI EFESTO ALL'OLIMPO; 5° ANIMALI ED ESSERI FANTASTICI; 6° LOTTA DEI PIGMEI CONTRO LE GRU. SULLE ANSE:
ARTEMIS PERSICA E AIACE COL CADAVERE DI ACHILLE.

FURTW. REICHOLD, GRIECH. VASENMALEREI, TAV. 1 - 3 E 11 - 13.
HOPPIN, A HANDBOOK OF BLACK-FIGURED VASES, PAG. 160 SEGG.
(CIRCA 570 A. C.)

9

▶

The "Milani Apollo": Greek kouros from the VIth century B.C., the name from the possessor, director of the Museum in the last century.

Cinerary Urns from Chiusi, IIth century B.C.
1. Lid representing a Lasa (Etruscan demon of death) which spreads its wing over the defunct.
2. The "Mater Matuta" (Italic goddess of dawn): the 'divinized' defunct with her son on her lap.

the situation, it might be the hero-ized defunct in a necropolis. Sometimes it was an 'ex-voto' of the offerer who in this way dedicated his person near a temple; or else a famous athlete to consecrate to the admiration of posterity in the location of the games. The anatomic characteristics: refined hair style, the analytical representation of the musculature and the articulation, the slight flection of the arm... But above all, and beyond the details, the body as a combination and synthesis of simple geometric solids date this work to the archaic period not later than the last decades of the 6 th century B.C.

The "Apollino" Milani presents different characteristics: more evocative than the large *Kouros*, it is a pursuit of grace and harmony more than of strength – contrary to its powerful companion. Substituting the rigorous constitution of geometric forms, there is instead softer modelling with the muscles subtly emerging under the skin and there are tenuous chiaroscuro (light/dark) effects. Such qualities date the work towards the end of the 6th century B.C.

From the grant of the daughter of the great archaeologist, Elisa, there is on display for the first time in a public museum the 'Relief of the Niobes'. It is a roman copy in reduced dimensions of the frieze from the throne of Zeus in Olympia, one of the most celebrated of antiquity, where Phidias had executed the chryselephantine statue of Zeus (in gold and ivory like the Athena Parthenos of the Parthenon). They were such a success in Rome to become a source of inspiration in the various workshops of *marmorarii* (marble workers) and were copied numerous times. Based on these reproductions and according to the testimony of historians, we present a reconstruction at the side of the page.

We find the same theme (the sons of Leto, Apollo and Artemis who shoot arrows at the sons of Niobe) among the favorites in antiquity for the drama of the scene: e.g. the room of the Niobe in the Uffizi, commissioned by the Lorrain Grand dukes to house the statues of the hellenistic period.

In the following room...

The sarcophagus of Larthia Seianti, wife of

1

2

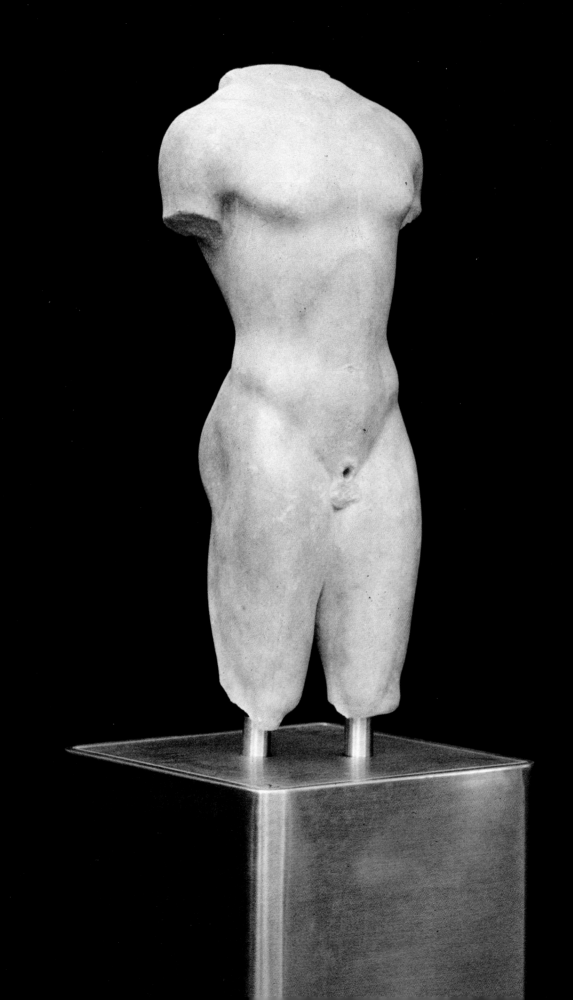

The "Milani Apollino": Greek kouros, later work than the "Apollo" of the proceeding illustration, from the Milani collection.

Relief of the Niobes: Roman reproduction, of the Hellenistic period, from the frieze of the Throne of Zeus in Olympia.

Svenia, found in Chiusi, is decorated with rosettes alternated with pilasters and is an example again of the vivacious decoration in polychromy absorbed by the terracotta during the baking.

The matron presents herself to the gods of the Inferi with her toilette completed, showing off an actual *parure* (set) composed of crown/cone earrings, necklace with a winged head of Medusa, bracelets, a belt with gold threadings, even five rings (two on the ring-finger and none on the index) on her left hand which holds a plate; she is probably applying herself with a touch of a perfumed unguent.

The heavy jewelry, symbolic of her social standing, do not do more than accentuate still further the interior emptiness, evident in the idleness of her stance and the inexpressiveness of her gaze.

The ostentation of comfort and ease is also manifest in the funerary furnishings where together with the customary unguents and objects of her toilette, there is included an "asse onciale" (an ancient roman money that was divided into twelve 'once'). It is not the usual "obolo" (obolus, coin) with Charon – for the ferryboat – but a coin of value of the roman series with a singular multiple, the silver denarius (10 assi) and even five lower multiples of a more current usage.

Sarcophagus of Larthia Seianti, from Chiusi, 2nd half of IInd century B.C.; in terracotta with rich polychrome decoration; on the lid, the defunct making herself up; on the chest, decoration in rosettes and pilasters.

The dating is determined between the Lex Papiria (217 B.C. introduction of the'asse onciale' of 27 grams) and the Lex Flaminia (89 B.C. semi-onciale asse). Based on the stylistic characteristics it dates back to the first half of the 2nd century B.C.

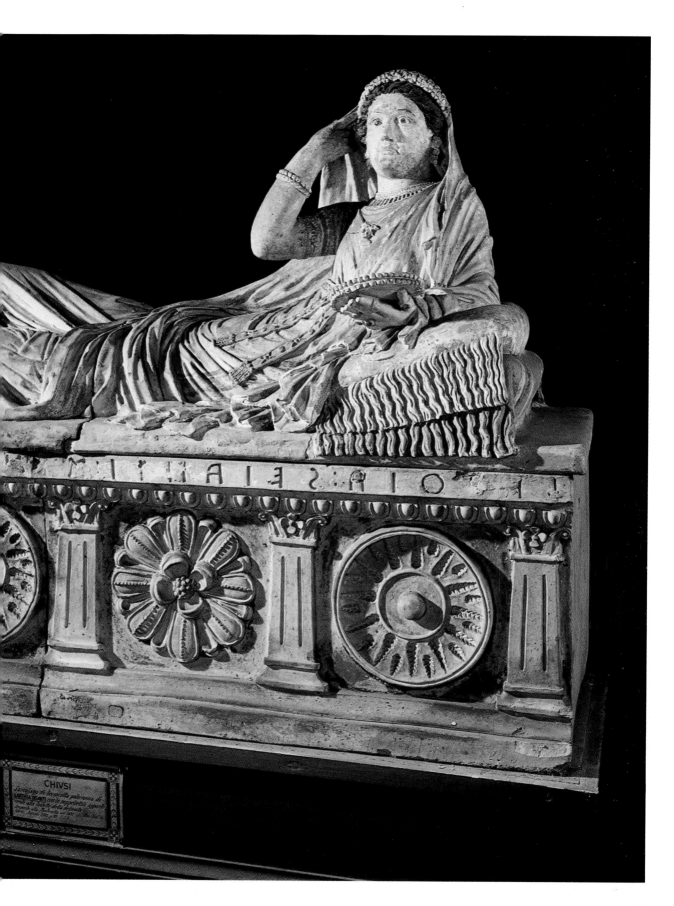

15

The first floor

The Room of the Urns: opposite the Sarcophagus of the Amazons; on the walls, urns from Volterra in alabaster; from Chiusi in terracotta; from Perugia in tufaceous stone.

Room of the urns

From the enormous Volterra production of cinerary alabaster urns various examples are conserved here. The simplest present decoration with geometric motifs or stylized flowers, fantastic animals (Scille or Grifons), heads of Gorgons, Lase (winged demons of death). Typical of the Volterra style is the scene of the parting between the newlyweds and the other members of the family, which usually takes place in front of a slightly open door to the Inferi or in front of a funerary cippus (trunk of a pilaster without capital, usually with an inscription, serving various ways esp. as sepulchral monument), often in the presence of a hellish demon: Charun, Tuchulcha or a Lasa. These same demons, the first having been mutated from Greek mythology, the others typical of the Etruscan world, accompany the defunct with the retinue and the insignia of his office or function, on his trip to the Inferi on foot, on horseback, on a chariot or a cart, sometimes by boat.

The urns with episodes from Greek mythology are of a better artistic quality with more elaborate and complex scenes (trojan cycle, Theban, heroic, with a preference for the more tragic or cruel episodes) that clearly prevail in the tombs of the great noble families and that obviously indicate an economic advantage. But above all they are proof of the penetration in the dominating classes of a cultural

model which had become symbol of social prestige.

On the lids the male defunct is represented reclining on the *Kline* with his left arm while the right hand holds a Patera, a *Tabula scriptoria*, a cornucopia, sign of abundance. The female defunct holds a fan, a mirror or a pomegranate intepreted as symbol of fecundity; the name is usually engraved on the lid. The physical traits are more or less stylized, but sometimes it is a true portrait often of extraordinary expressionism.

There are no two alabaster urns alike; from the similarity of the composition one deduces the existence of a 'cartoon' (design) being part of an actual album, a repertoire of subjects from which the patron made his choice. The artist, however, with the best intuition, adds or subtracts a figure, varies the detail or changes a pose, enriches or diminishes the composition.

Among these, on the center shelf below, to the right of the entrance, an urn which belonged, according to tradition, to Michelangelo; the decoration shows soldiers who lift a killed companion onto a cart. The abandon of the dead soldier and the arching of the bodies of his companions strained in their struggle, might have inspired the maestro (Michelangelo) for the Pietà of S. Marie del Fiore and the Pietà Rondanini. While a more credible reference is sought in the Pietà of Palestrina, even though of dubious authenticity.

Among the urns in terracotta from Chiusi extracted from a singular mold and painted orginally in bright polychrome, two scenes of armed struggle are frequently repeated: a duel between soldiers one of which succumbs and flanked by two Lase: it is difficultly interpreted as the duel between Heteoclus

Chiusi Urns from the same workshop, IInd century B.C.

Urn of Larth Purni Curce: Battle between Etruscans and Gauls.

the city of Pieve, 2nd centry B.C. Battle bewteen Etruscans and Gauls.

In the center a Gaul with a *torque* round his neck is killed by an Etruscan soldier while two cavaliers, one with rich armor, gallop in different directions and trample two Gauls. It is the typical example of Hellenistic art characterized by a pursuit for drama in the poses and the expressions of the figures. The composition is an excellent example of the ability to variate a fairly conventional scheme.

and Polynices for the throne of Thebes in somuch as both die and the father Oedipus is missing.

A soldier armed with a plow is in combat with three enemies in the presence of a Lasa: it is the Greek hero Echetlos who, sprung forth from the earth during the battle of Marathon, was swallowed by earth after having massacred persian soldiers. The legend was readily accepted in Etruria where the myth of Tagete existed: a boy with the wisdom of an elder – he too sprung forth from the earth – who revealed the rituals for honoring the gods.

The Urn of Larth Purni Curce is in alabaster from

Urn of Arnth Purni Curcesa

In the center of the chest, Caco, a seer and singer, with an inspired and absorbed air about him and the lyre in his hand to accompany his song, does not realize he is about to be attacked by armed soldiers. Next to him, a companion begs for mercy. (The same scene is reproduced on the urn with lion feet to the left of the entrance door to the next room). The two soldiers who begin to attack them are Aulo and Celio Vibenna, known from a mirror engraved with the same subject and the names of the figures. The two heroes are known as the companions of

Urn of Arnth Purni Curcesa: Avlo and Celio Vibenna who attack the seer Caco.

characteristics seem to belong to the same workshop and date from the 2nd century B.C.

In the center: Sarcophagus of Ramtha Huzcnai Thuiati known as the "Sarcophagus of the Amazons", in Asia Minor marble in polychrome tempera from Tarquinia. On the long sides of the sarcophagus: two quadrighe (two-wheeled chariots) (Page 21) guided by Amazons who assail four greek soldiers of whom the two armed with lances in the center resist, and the other two succumb. One of

Mastarna who became king of Rome with the name of Servio Tullio: in the pictures of the François of Vulci Tomb, where substituting the greeks who stab the trojan prisoners are the above-mentioned etruscan soldiers who kill the romans, among whom Cneo Tarquinio from Rome, the etruscan version of the event is represented. Nothing is known of the episode to which the scene of the urn alludes, but is certain proof of the existence of an etruscan epic with as protagonists the Vibenna brothers and which Roman history has willingly left out or ably counterfeited.

The urns of the two Purni with similar typological

the escaping Amazons is attacked by three greek soldiers on each side, they in turn assaulted on each side by Amazons on horseback. (Page 20) On the short side two Amazons attack a greek soldier while from the other side a greek wounds an Amazon aided by a companion.

It is a work by a greek artist or at least an artist working in greek style and active around the middle of the 5th century B.C. It is exceptional in the pursuit of diverse rhythms still maintaining a symmetry in the composition, the ability in the execution of the perspectives or shots, in the effects of movement, in the confident line and the rich

Sarcophagus of Ramtha Huzcnai Thuiati, from Tarquinia, probably a work by a Greek artist, in marble painted with polychrome tempera, IVth century B.C.

Amazons on horseback against Greek warriors.

coloring. The modelling does not correspond to the high quality of the painting; it is instead of an archaic taste seen in the Atteone chewed by the lions, in the lateral tympanums, for which one supposes a lapse between the execution of the sarcophagus and that of the painted scenes done later.

Sarcophagus with Battle between Greeks and Gauls

The sober stylization of the defunct reclined on the *kline* with a back or headboard is of a surprising modernness in the full articulation of the masses from the fusiform appendages of the fingers culminating in the oval head. It contrasts with the chaotic scene of a battle described in minute detail and vitalized by the oblong shields with the participation of winged Lase. The absence of decoration on the short sides and the overall existence of rough hewn marks indicate an unfinished work, perhaps because of irregular and non-homogeneous ';tufacea' stone.

To the left of the entrance, in the cabinet at the door: urn of *Arnth Velsi Cencu Vesialisa* from, Chiusi; to the "Tria Nomina" which would also be the roman (praenomen, gens, cognomen) is added to explicate: "of the son of Vesi".

It represents an episode from the final part of Orestea which seems to have penetrated fairly late

Chariot of Amazons galloping.

in etruscan art and was represented only in the Chiusi environment. The urns from Sarteano in the Archaeological Museum of Siena with "variants" and another smaller in Berlin are by the same hand or workshop.

The two inseparable friends Orestes and Pilade, captured by Toante, king of Tauride, and condemned for having tried to steal the statue of Artemis, are waiting to be sacrificed. On that occasion Iphigenia, a priestess, recognizes her brother. On the right a maid who carries an umbilicated patera with fruits for the libations, holds back a cry of emotion. Iphigenia seeks and consoles Orestes who is distraught due to his cruel destiny

and because of his remorse for his matricide. Pilade, with his wrists tied, turns to comfort him and holds the *Pugillares* (tablets-letters) by means of which brother and sister will recognize each other. He is threatened by one of the Erinyes (Furies) who has chased Orestes from the moment of his crime with unsheathed swords.

The last figure on the right is a *pendant* added for symetry. On the one hand, the scene is an example of greek mythology misconceived: the clothing of the maid is all wrong with the loin-cloth and the crossed bands which is typical of the Erinyes, while the figure on the right simply fills in for equilibrium in the composition. It reaches, however, a high

Urn of Arnth Velsi Cencu Vesialisa, in alabaster from Chiusi. On the chest, Orestes' recognition of Tauride: a Greek myth in the interpretation of an Etruscan artist.

aesthetic level because of the clean division, enhanced by the cippus surmounted by the lebete, between two moments of unequal *pathos*: on the left the two nude bodies barely touch in tender contact creating an atmosphere of desolate resignation and thoughtful intimacy. On the right the armed figures take on the conventional attitude and dynamic of the tragic repertoire. The two scenes, one composed and the other a spontaneous instant 'photograph', stand out one to the other.

Even the portrait on the lid has a

The "Obese One": Lid of a sarcophagus in alabaster from Chiusi, end of the IIIrd century B.C. Physical opulence and inertia of a culture in decline, the "Obesus Etruscus" of Carme XXXIX of Catullo.

well-characterized physiognomy.

Room of the Funerary Monuments

Objects of various origin dealing with the funerary cult are on display in this room. On the left the series of alabaster funerary urns continues. In the center a peperino sarcophagus decorated with lions, grifons and masks from Orvieto, and an archaic sphinx from Tuscania.

One of the most famous pieces of etruscan sculpture (on the left wall next to the entrance) is the "Sarcophagus of the Obese One" in alabaster from Chiusi from the end of the 3rd century B.C.

The pose of the banqueter with the patera, the ring and the necklace is conventional; the corpulence, sign of opulence, is particularly accentuated and expressed here in calm undulating rhythms. But beyond the typical 'picturesqueness' of the ostentation of so much paunch, it is the physiognomy of the figure that is remarkable: well characterized in the thinning at the temples, in the subtle but sensual mouth, in the aquiline nose. He expresses a sense of pitiful tiredness, as an extinguishing of vitality and creativity. One can not help but think that the roman conquest of Etruria has already happened at the end of the 3rd century B.C., in his grave melancholy he seems to express a resigned acquiescence to the will of Fate; the end of the Etruscan people would be promised just a few *saecula* from then. He is the wealthy man, the

Urn reproducing the Etruscan house, with arched doorway and 'bugnato'. From Chiusi, IVth century B.C.

conquered, under the new barbarians.

There is on the right side of the room, above, the corner of the frontespiece of a tomb from the rocky necropolis of Norchia (Viterbo) sawn by the most able and furtive thieves and only recuperated in the last century (the remaining part was left on site). The scene shows a wounded soldier being moved. In the middle the double door of a Chiusi tomb; also, a sepulchral lion keeps watch over a tomb, of neafro, from Bolsena; and an archaic sphinx of tufo (stone) from Tuscania.

The tomb was usually distinguished by a cippus in the form of a crown, like those along the wall of the door, flanked by archaic statues of the "daedalean type".

The most interesting finds, apart from moulded cinerary terracotta urns from Chiusi, are on display on the wall.

Urn in the form of an etruscan house: it presents a sloping roof with stylized flower decoration, a low open gallery, a large arched door enframed by smooth cut ashlar (stone blocks) and ionic pilasters, missing on the long sides, which support a *dolium*. This is a pitcher used since antiquity as a container for foodstuffs; on can assume that it served, along with an oil burning torch, to mark the entrance way.

Urn with Banquet Scene, decorated with 'drip' decoration in bronze, from Chiusi, end of VIth century B.C.

The use of the round arch, typical of etruscan architecture and a fundamental element of roman construction, as well as the use of the ashlar, one sees incorporated again in the construction of the florentine renaissance palace.

On the left side: urn with a banquet scene from Chiusi, 6th century B.C. It is decorated with a series of bronze drip stones in the shape of a lioness *protome*. The two basreliefs represent on one side a banquet scene with two male couples and their servants next to them, while a dog and a goose await the scraps under the tables. The utilization of small cornices (ledges) attached to the walls, also

documented from the paintings of the triclinio tomb of Tarquinia, was still common at the beginning of this century in the tuscan countryside. On the other side, a series of dancers in stylized poses, these too quite similar to the tarquinian paintings.

Room of the Bronzes

The Etruscans have been praised in particular for their exploitation of the mines. All their territory was rich in minerals (the Colline Metallifere, Elba Island and the Campigliese in Tuscany; the Tolfa

► **Etruscan bronze head of the Hellenistic period from the Galleries. (presently not on display)**

Roman bronze head from the Imperial age from the Galleries. (presently not on display)

and Allumiere mountains in Lazio).

They were also celebrated for their workmanship with these metals which was already advanced in the archaic epoch and evermore perfected thanks to an intense commercial network of exchange/trade and the consequent acquisition of new techniques. It is not rare to find metal products of etruscan manufacture over all the Mediterranean area. Their principal wealth was iron (the gigantc slag heaps in Populonia are the proof) but they also possessed the primary materials for making bronze: copper and tin. The lost-wax method was the technique for the fusion; also practiced by the greeks and romans, it was left practically unaltered through the centuries. It is explained here summarily.

Within an iron framework a statue in clay was modelled which when baked, loses its dampness. At this point the artist had a statue of terracotta which he covered with a layer of wax. Then he proceeded with the actual finishing or detail.

The next step was to cover the clay and wax figure with another layer of clay inserting tubes or 'cannule' with an external mouth into which the molten bronze will later be poured. In the meantime with another baking the wax melts and escapes through these tubes. The molten bronze was then poured and filling in, forces the air to escape and occupies the inner space and shape once held by the wax. Once all is cooled and hardened the external terracotta mould is broken and the inner substance is eliminated: thus producing a statue with less bronze and of lighter weight.

In the glass cabinets are numerous small votive bronzes, from the more archaic in stiff frontal poses similar to the greek *kouroi*, to the more recent figures in more natural stance. They present the typical gesture of the offerer who tilts the patera making a libation to the god, or that of the orator with his right or both hands lifted in the act of praying – a gesture typical of the first Christians documented in the paintings of the catacombs. The figures usually have no base in that they were normally displayed on wooden stands and periodically gathered up and deposited in a votive cabinet near the sacred place. Some of the little bronzes, still from the votive cabinets, represent the sacrificed animal.

Also on display are different parts of furniture decoration in bronze; legs, corner, angular and frontal plaques and candelabra crowns. On the right of the entrance is the handle of a cista, a cylindrical receptacle with a lid, with decoration interesting for the subject albeit common in etruscan art, and showing two soldiers carrying a deceased comrade.

Proceding from the left, the remains of a group from Chianciano (known since antiquity for the thermal mineral water) from a temple probably dedicated to a god of health.

The fragments belonged to an archaic Apollo (6th cent.) here with a part of the shoulder and headdress with an opening at the nape of the neck

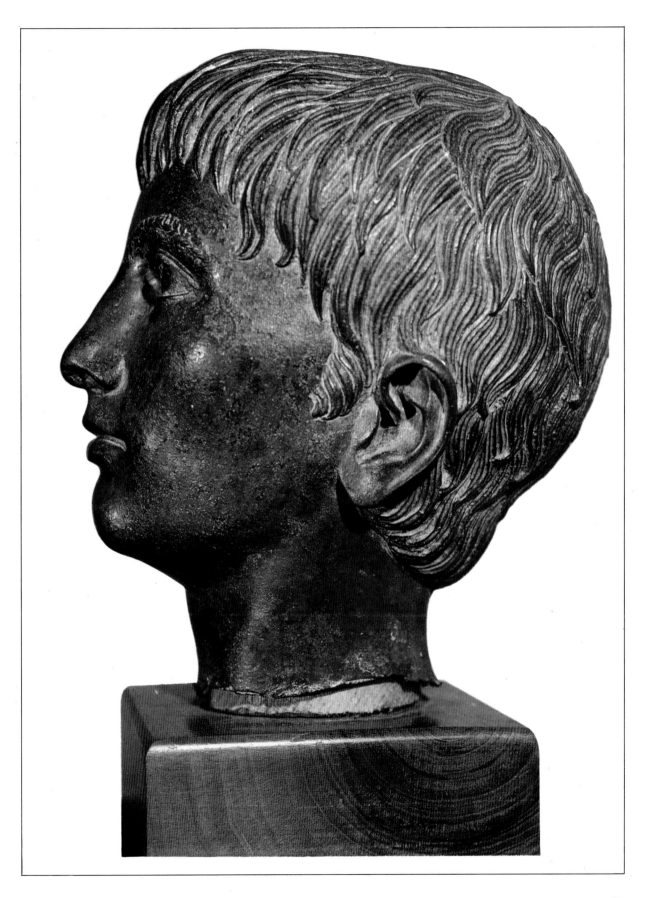

The "Idolino": Original Greek bronze of the Vth century B.C., or a later roman copy from the Medici collection; it represents a youth in the act of completing an offering.

Christian lantern from the IVth century A.D. with Paul at the bow preaching and Peter at the rudder. in the inscription on the mast: "Dominus legem/Dat Valerio Severo/Eutropi Vivas": "The Lord gives the Law to Valerio Severo – best wishes to Eutropio" Probably a gift to Valerio Severo who took on with baptism the name Beneaugurale (best wishes or blessing) of Eutropio, (or that which turns to good).

The back of an engraved mirror from Populonia; a warrior, Laran, together with another warrior, Celsclan, unarmed and without helmet, threatens him with a sword. (presently not on display)

probably for the insertion of an oil lamp so that the eyes (made of glass) would glow and the statue would be animated. Also a cart, here with the rod of the shaft, for Silena-Diana, indentifiable observing the half-moon and sceptre, her traditional symbols with another male statue.

The Minerva of Arezzo found in a well under the church of San Lorenzo in 1554:

It is a copy of the Hellenistic period from the original in marble by Praxiteles of the 4th century B.C. known by the many roman copies which present it with the right arm against the body holding a lance. Only the bust to the fold under the breast is authentic; the rest is from a rather interpretive and liberal restoration. It is the typical statue destined to be an object of cult, of a stately solemnity. At the nape of the neck where the hair begins, there is a circular opening much too small

for an oil lamp: one can hypothesize that it served as an aperture for an inserted tube through which one shouted fearful prophesies which echoed within this bronze cavity.

The Chimera

The story of one of the most famous masterpieces of etruscan art deserves to be remembered. Its discovery in Arezzo in 1554 during the construction of the city fortifications near the rampart of San

Lorentino was sensational among the artists and writers of the time. Tradition tells us that the restoration, not easily identifiable today, was placed in the charge of Cellini who in any case does not talk about it in his autobiography. The tail was missing at the time of discovery as the contemporary drawings reveal.

Displayed in Palazzo Vecchio, in the room of Leo X (where it has since returned in occasion of the Medici Exhibitions) the statue acquired a political value: they were the monstrous enemies of the *pax ducalis* that Cosimo I had had to combat and defeat in order to construct and consolidate his new state which would then be called Etruria, while the decorations in 'grottesca style', rich with fantastic

▶

The Chimera of Arezzo: found in 1554, once belonging to the Medici collection. It subsequently underwent a 'freely interpreted' restoration; an Etruscan bronze from between the Vth and IVth centuries B.C., it was probably part of a group. It is represented in the act of hurling itself upon the hero Bellerofonte.

The "Arringatore": a late Etruscan bronze, found in 1566 at Sanguineto on the Lake Trasimeno, once in the Medici collection. It represents an orator who asks for silence. In the iscription on the hem of the toga, the dedication to Aulo Metello, son of Vel and Vesi.

animals and designed by Vasari, would then be its natural 'frame'. It is in fact Vasari, in a writing regarding his 'inventive' decorations, who testifies that the "lion" is identified as the mythical Chimera ("goat" in Greek) based on a comparision with the animal represented in the coin of Sicione, a city of the Peloponnesus, in the Medici collection of medals. In this the tail darts upwards describing an "s" certainly as in the original.

After its transferal to the Uffizi in 1718, the tail was added by Spinazzi in 1785, erroneously in the act of biting the horn on the head of the goat which emerges from the back.

The beast was probably a part of a group, and is represented in the act of hurling against Bellerofonte who, one imagines, is incumbent on the winged horse Pegasus and who has already inflicted two mortal wounds to the bowed neck of the goat, and one to the rear paw.

The inscription TINSCVIL on the right paw is the dedication: a votive offering to TIN (the roman Jupiter).

The genious of the artist is evident: he captures the moment of preparation of the action in which the feline's body contracts in a spasm of pain preparing for the jump, is full of a contained violence and tense in his extreme will to survive. The wriggling veins under the taut skin are realistic as are the contracted paws with the nails projecting. Instead the wrinkles of the muzzle around the open jaws are stylized as is the mane with 'flaming' locks. This stylistic symbiosis makes the dating difficult, varying between the 5th and 4th centuries B.C.

The "Arringatore" (the 'haranguer') from Sanguineto on Lake Trasimeno from the beginning of the 1st century B.C.: It was named by the Abbot Lanzi in 1789 and is thus known.

It is a statue of an orator wearing a short toga and high sandals of natural size, captured in the firm gesture of one who demands silence from the auditorium with sure authority.

The inscription in the hem of the toga, according to the translation by P. Bernardini Marzolla in the text already cited, is thus interpreted: "To Aule Meteli, son of Vel and Vesi, that this statue would establish the assembly thanks to the public contribution". A well-deserving personality, not known other than by name: the powerful Metelli

were aristocratic etruscans and then romans in an Etruria already conquered, who in those years (89 B.C.) obtain roman citizenship. The sense of *dignitas* in the imperial and solemn attitude is roman, but there is also a strong, forceful sense of unrest in the imbalance in the forward lean, in the folds of the toga that have an upward thrust enfolding the prominent abdomen. A product worthy of the great etruscan realism, it is positive expression of an art that manages to free itself from the greek influence but which here is charged with a new tension. This noble etruscan is again powerful

33

in Rome but this time with a sense of melancholic
regret for a culture destined to be contaminated in
the loss of identity of its people.

From the corridor of bronzes which looks onto
the garden where various types of etruscan tombs
have been reconstructed (on the right, the tomb of
the little devil of Vetulonia in a square-shape with a
dome supported by angular spandrels) one enters a
room with various funerary furnishings. In the
cabinet on the left, above, military equipment with
axes, lance tips, umboni (the 'umbilical' of the
round shield) and halfmoon razors typical of male
tombs. Below, domestic equipment or tools with
jars and ktichen utensils not so different from our
own. In the cabinet on the left, tools for work in the
fields, pitchers and candelabra usually crowned by a
little statue with points to put the candles on.

In the center, a situla (the great grandfather of
our copper pitcher) in bronze with the return of
Hephaestus from Olympia; and an elegant oil-lamp
base with the head of a winged Medusa encircled by
an inscription with a typical dedication which
explains that it was part a funerary group of
decoration of the Velthuri family.

▶
View of the garden.

Corinthian Olpe with zoomorphic decoration in bands from the first half of the IVth century B.C.... and its Etruscan imitation: substituting Greek elegance and sobriety, one sees here the fantasy and the decorative richness of an Etruscan artist.

The first rooms of the second floor organized according to the 19th century museum criteria, present heterogeneous finds to offer a picture, rich in comparative terms, of a singular geographical, italic or mediterranean area.

Mesopotamian and Cyprian Antiquity

Because of the scarcity of tablet material, the common writing material is terracotta on which one impresses or rolls (slides) over with a seal in hard stone, as a "signature"; rather curious is the unopened "letter" with the text summarized on the envelope in cuneiform characters.

Among the cyprian antiquities there is ceramic with elegant geometric decoration following natural shapes.

Room of the Greek, Etruscan, Italic and Roman Vases.

From room 7, continuing to the right through the

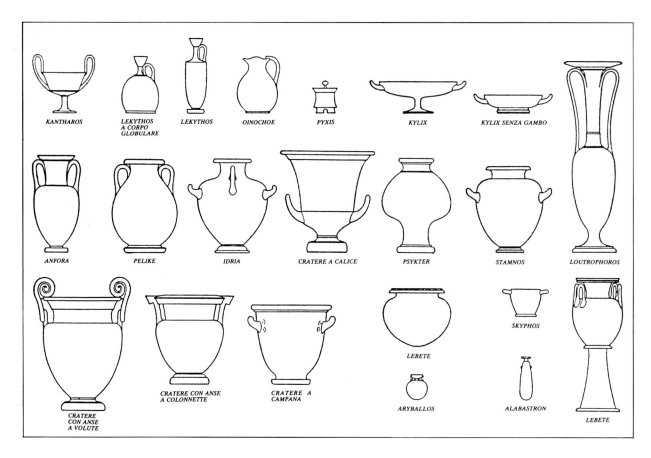

Molds of Greek Vases

rooms 11, 12, 13 and 14, one can follow the stages of the greek vase painting, its imitations and differentiations in the etruscan and italic painting up until the roman production of the republican and imperial ages. The dates, when otherwise not indicated, refer to the period Before Christ. It is preferred to provide here the essential characteristics of each style instead of a singular examination of each of the finds – which are illustrated with the captions – in order to make a chronological picture of a long-term scale stand out in a continuous overview, and with the most significant examples which can be integrated by the charts provided in each room.

Apart from the styles, the technique remains the same: the artist proceeds by tracing the outline of the design with a fine point on the vase – which was previously smoothed over using a damp cloth – Then it was immersed in a ochre "bath"; the coloring pigment is essentially constituted of ferric oxide. The baking is done in 3 phases: in the first, in the presence of oxygen, the painted parts take on a red color; in the second, without oxygen, the same parts assume a black color; in the third phase, of short duration, the parts painted with just one or light coats of paint become red again while those parts with several coats remain black.

Room VII – Greek and Etruscan Vases

In the first three centuries of the first millennium vases are with a decoration in bands minutely filled with geometric designs in various ways and with rare forms or figures also stylized and reduced to refined schemes, usually funereal processions (typical those of Dipylon of Athens). It was succeeded in the 8th century, with the center in Corinth, a production of eastern inspiration: the decoration is constituted of horizontal bands with long series of animals, plants and flowers all stylized as border, and graffito design. One can determine quite precisely the date according to the evolution of the constant details (for example, the rose which is gradually modified). In contrast to the corinthian eastern style, the ceramics of Attica introduce the figures on a red background touched up with white lead (see François vase) and which usually reserve the central

Attica Pelike from the IVth century B.C. with scenes of the market: 1. A vendor offers a taste of his oil, exalting the quality: "KALON EĨ" – "Good, isn't it?"
2. A potter shoos away two dogs which are fighting and threatening the safety of his merchandise, where one vase is already broken: "KUNR(AI)EMI" – "Dog, break me!"
(interpretation of C. Guarnieri)

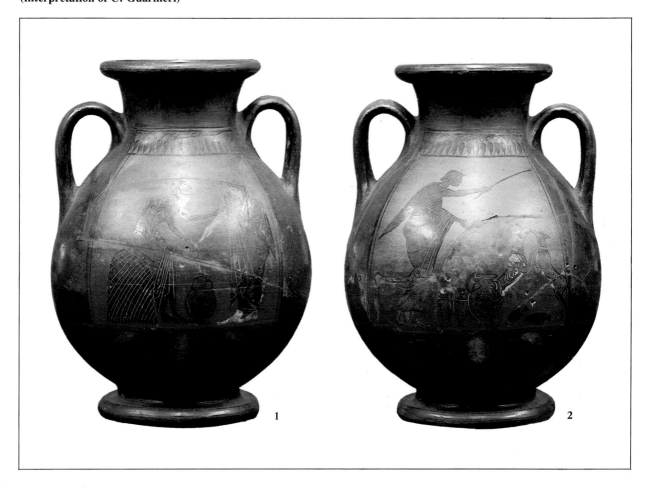

part of the vase for a scene and leave the zoomorphic (or phytomorphic) decoration in the secondary parts. The Attica style, much less attached to rigid schemes, soon acquired the Mediterranean market including the Etruscan, so much so that the factories or workshops of Corinth were forced to conform and even imitate the style. The krater or bowl in the center of the room on little columns is from the late Corinthian period; and it has red ingubbiatura bringing it closer to the Attica production.

Quite soon the Etruscans imitated the greek styles (towards the end of the 7th century), but without the precision and accuracy in their models, yet often with a greater capability for fantasy. In the cabinets on the right at the side of the door, the Etruscans' imitations distinguished themselves for their lighter tone or color of the clay. For a more precise comparison, take for example the olpe (pitcher with round mouth inventory number 3722) of Corinthian production and the similar Etruscan one (inven. number 71022).

Room XI – Vases with black figures on a red background

The vases with black figures on a red background

37

are from the first style of the Attica ceramic works: the figures in black stand out on the orange background with the details of anatomy and the drapery in graffiti and with touches of white and red. They were of the Attica production but destined for the Etruscan market and were the so-called tyrrhenian vases from the middle of the 6th century. Found mostly in the southern part of Etruria, they usually present a central scene and keep the decoration in bands of an eastern corinthian taste – in keeping with the Etruscan preference of fantastic over rational. Also on display, one of the oldest examples (c. 550) of a panathenaeaic amphora which was given to the athletic victor as a prize in the Panatenee contest, a celebration in honor to Athena which took place each year (the little Panatenee) and every four years (the "large" one) which culminated the 28 th of July. On one side is represented the image of the goddess and on the other the victors in battle and the writing, "prize for the games of Athena". In this example there is the chariot race. These amphorae continue the technique of the black figures even later and then it was abandoned. A more traditional approach (as apposed to an inventive one) suits the scene of the ritual games awards which was a cult-related event. They did include however, generic lively scenes, true *trannhes de vie*, like in the pelike where a potter shoos two dogs away with a whip; they were fighting and thus threatening the welfare of his merchandise.

Room XII – Vases with red figures on black background

Around 530 there came about an opposite procedure: the entire surface of the vase is filled-in in black leaving the figures uncovered, designing the details in black but no longer in graffito – instead with a fine brush and therefore the line became much softer and clean.

The technique of red figures on black background became the most successful and dominated for about a century and a half with various phases which here are described essentially.

The first generation of painters who adopted this style (530-490) still show traces in the rigid line of the preceeding style: the musculature is reduced, often schematic, with head and legs in profile. But the peplos wool which drapes heavily has already been substituted with the soft linen chitone with more elegant and tighter folds. The decoration is of palms and flowers. The transitions to the 2nd generation (c. 500-475) is characterized by the appearance of meander (the so-called "greek"; greek fret or key pattern) while the eye, earlier represented frontally, is shown in profile with the pupil in the same direction as the gaze. It is the form of the eye, in fact, still in profile but now open in the interior, which marks aproximately the transition to the 3rd generation in a search for more natural or varied or, in certain cases, more dramatic poses (475-450). It is also the period in which painting on large surfaces flourishes. Today completely lost, in antiquity they were more prized than sculpture. Among others, the names of Micone and Polignoto come down to us who decorated the Stoa Pecile of Athens. We can have only an idea of this from the vase painting, as they were in compositions on a vast scale that would be doubtfully conceived for the reduced surface of a vase. Around the mid 5th century and up to 420 (the third generation) we see a return to more monumental and tempered poses, perhaps because of the influence of the friezes by Phidias in the Parthenon in Athens in the age of Pericles in the apogee of his power.

The period between the 4th and 5th centuries there were attempts of perspective but limited to small objects: the figures are placed against different planes and light/dark (chiaroscuro) effects are used, while the retouching in gold is present after the first half of the century. The most representative painter of this style (the so-called "Fiorito" 'flowered' after the "Severo" 'severe', and the "Nobile" noble) is Meidias whose two marvelous Hydrie the museum possesses; they were a precious *pendant* of an etruscan house (and come from Populonia). The subjects, the choice of which is already in itself significant, are taken from the circle or court of Aphrodite who is accompanied in one by Phaonis and in the other by Adonis with his retinue of winged cupids and surrounded by figures personifying the amenities of life. The graceful gestures, the often languid, relaxed poses in the

Attica Hydria by the painter of Meidias, from Populonia
from the end of the Vth century B.C.: Meeting of the gods,
among whom Faone who plays the lyre, from the circle of
Aphrodite who flies on high on a chariot pulled by Eroti.

'Krater' of "the Argonauts": Etruscan imitation of Attica ceramics from the IVth century B.C.; 'freely interpreted' and inspired from a Greek paintig of vast dimension. From the Galleries.

figures with their drapery wrapped around their bodies in sinuous folds, the minute line of the design united with the gold retouching, the sobriety of the details which suggest space rather than represent it: all this prove this painter to be an exquisite example of refined skill.

Contemporarily to the production of red figures, the LEKYTHOI or vases of small dimensions were being produced. They were of an elongated form with a high neck, painted black like the foot with

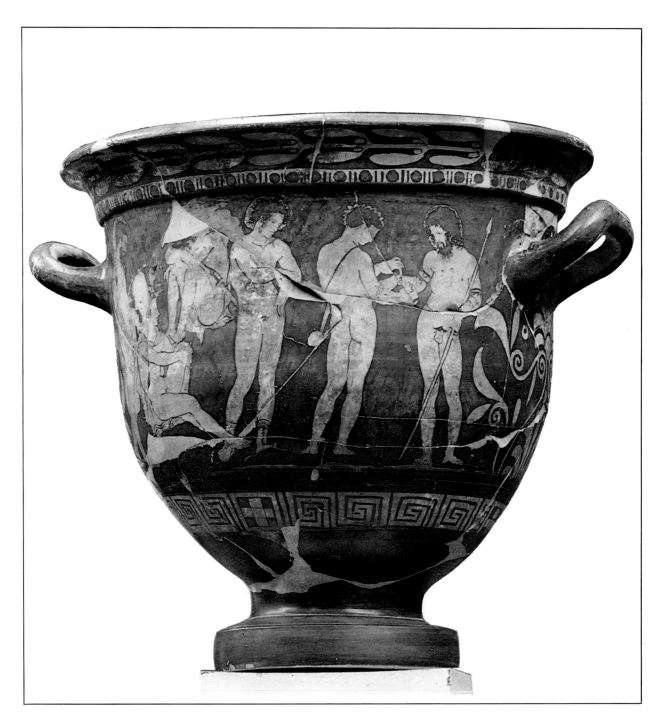

polychrome decoration. They usually represent a funerary ceremony and were filled with perfumed oil and offered to the defunct. On the vases for the most part are nude figures designed with the utmost finesse; they were then "dressed" by the artist. Because of the disappearance of the polychromy, the pure design of the nude limited to the outline is left and is today extremely evocative.

Room XIII – Etruscan and Italic Vases

While the Attica production fell into decline in the 4th century, there was in the continental part of Magna Grecia the apula production characterized by monumental forms with rich decoration painted in stylized floral motifs and polychrome scenes. The themes are taken from daily life (common the matron who is doing her toilet) or from the dionysian cult (figures of the court such as satyrs and maenads or bacchante) or, as in the krater with volutes on the right, scenes of offering near the little temple of the deceased hero. Less often the scenes are of a duel or in any case cruel. It is a 'provincial' genre of a rather heavy and elaborate taste and undoubtably originating from models from the mother country which manages all the same to go beyond imitation reaching its own unmistakable autonomy. Substituting a polychromy of the central scenes to the clear prevalence for design, this brings it closer to great wall painting rather than vase painting from the mother country. On the left there is Taranto ceramic and ceramic of the 2nd half of the 4th century. Still following the greek style but rielaborated according to etruscan sensibilities, the vases of Volterra and Perugia production are usually kraters on small columns.

In the center of the room the krater of the Argonauts, recognized as an imitation of greek ceramic by an etruscan. It presents on one side a series of male nudes in various easy and natural poses: one fastens a bracelet on another, one touches his arm, others watch or just relax. On the opposite side, a youth with a cape which leaves uncovered one shoulder is flanked by two women who look at him. The composition is clearly a derivation of a large greek painting, perhaps the return of the Argonauts painted by Micone towards

the end of the 5th century in the sanctuary of Dioscuri of which the admiring Pausania speaks. The original probably represents the heroes at rest intent in medicating each others' wounds or else taking care of their own bodies, captured in a serene atmosphere, saved from danger after the legendary venture. The quality of the paint certainly has nothing to do with greek precision, but the design is surely by a man of talent, close to that of the Cista Ficoroni in the Villa Giulia Museum in Rome.

Room XIV – Black and Aretine Ceramic

The ceramic completely painted black with decoration stamped or applied in relief is characteristic of the Roman Republican age and was produced throughout the italic peninsula and in Sicily between the end of the 4th and the 1st centuries. Its great success ensued of course, because it was a good imitation of bronze and much less expensive. In the beginning they were executed with care, but with time produced in series and often defective, produced with traces of finger prints/indentations at the foot of the piece due to the rapid painting by immersion, and irregularities in the baking because many were placed on top each other in the oven.

The Malacena production (location near Monteriggioni where vases of this type were found) maintained a high level of quality offering pieces with glossy and homogeneous paint with metalic reflections and exported from the zone of Volterra throughout the entire etruscan territory.

The red ceramic of Arezzo production called *terra sigillata* was produced in the smooth variation from c. 70 B.C. to 70 A.D. and in the decorative variation from c. 30 B.C. to 40 A.D. and reconciled elegance of form and decoration united at a good technical level with a low cost of production in series. It was obtained based on a matrix with decoration in the negative in the interior. On this is adhered the argil or clay which detaches almost by itself when shrinking due to the loss of humidity during the baking. The red paint is then applied by immersion. The most famous workshop is that of Perennio Bargate which presents a great variety of decorative motifs capable of satisfying the most

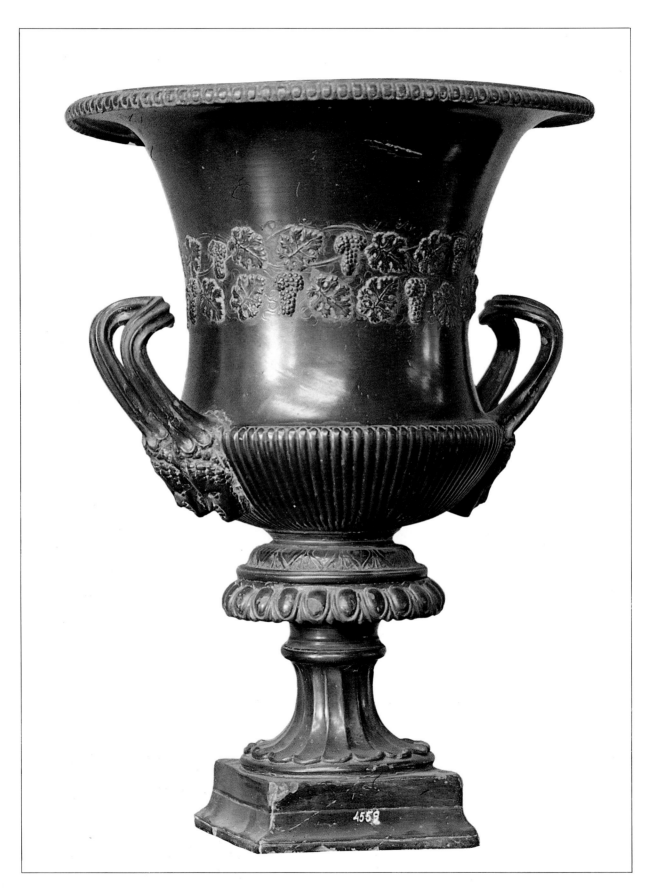

◄

'Krater' in black paint with printed decoration imitating bronze, typical of the Repulicam Roman period probably from the Etruscan production of Malacena.

Molds of Italic and Etruscan Vases

1 Vaso cinerario biconico Villanoviano; 2, 3 Kylix; 4 Vaso ad anello; 5 Alabastron; 6 Skyphos; 7, 8 Kyathos; 9, 10, 11 Calici; 12 Oinochoe; 13 Olpe; 14, 15 Kantharos.

Villanova tombs with bi-conical ossuaries with incised geometric decoration and with a bowl as a lid. In the cabinet to the right there is an urn which faithfully reproduces a rustic hut (note the holes for the smoke's draft): based on models of this type and utilizing the holes on site left from the supporting posts, it has been possible to reconstruct the humble shelter of the toscana/lazio countryside.

The following two rooms are dedicated to the "buccheri" (water vase), an exclusively etruscan

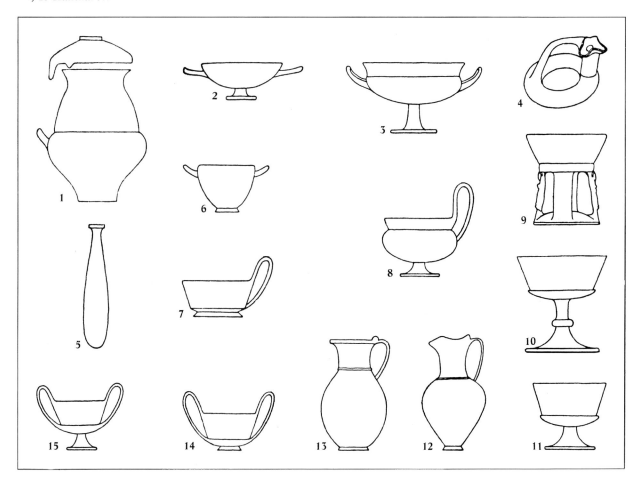

varied tastes of the roman public of the Empire: from the simple decoration of garlands of leaves, so elegant like those of the *Ara Pacis Augustae*, to the little cupids in various poses in refined taste like those of the Pompei house of the Vettii, to the skeletons in grotesque positions ("Memento mori"), or erotic scenes without meaning.

Rooms VIII, IX, X (To the left of room VII)

On display one finds the typical furnishings of the

production. It is a type of glossy black ceramic not painted, obtained by using purified clay rich in iron oxide, baked with the proper controls to isolate it from oxygen.

In the first room, dedicated to the light bucchero, it is quite common to find the decoration in little cylinders, a Chiusi production, obtained by rolling with pressure a matrix in the negative representing processions of fantastic animals and rites of the inferi or baccellature and fan motifs.

In the second room, the heavy bucchero (sometimes defined as the "barocco etrusco"). The motifs derive from the usual repertoire of oriental taste which the etruscan artist disengaged from greek rationality, interpreted and elaborated freely using these motifs without parsimony. The object was weighted with abundant decoration and the artist looked for new forms and created effects so unreal as to be magic. The oinochoe is unique in a fish form with a human protome, in the central cabinet; and there are various vases with bull heads.

Room XV – Votive and Architectonic Terracotta

This room presents some of the parts of the terracotta decoration of an etruscan temple.

Differing from the greek temple, in stone or marble, which is an example of harmony where each part is conceived relating one to the other and therefore admirable from every point of view, the etruscan temple was constructed instead in wood on a high platform with decoration nailed in terracotta. It is to be seen only frontally; while the Parthenon is a proportioned body, the temple of Talamone to which belonged the decoration on display in the museum, today in Orbetello, is a large body with an enormous and 'overloaded' head constituted of the fronton or pediment and the decoration in terracotta. There are examples left of this decoration originating from various locations with motifs taken from the traditional floral repertoire extracted from the matrices.

The votive terracotte representing parts of the human body respond to a popular religious requirement, still alive: the part of the body healed by God was dedicated to Him 'ex-voto' (as a votive offering). The difference between the external parts which were reproduced faithfully and the internal parts in an approximate anatomical way is quite obvious.

Usually the same votive cabinet presents like anatomical parts: in a Uni sanctuary (Juno Lucina "who gives light") the female genital is dedicated. The pieces on display here come from various locations in that they belonged for the most part to the Medici collections.

An 'Oinocoe' in the shape of a fish in heavy bucchero, decorated with a feminine protome: a singular example of the Etruscan "baroque" from the VIth century B.C.

THE EGYPTIAN MUSEUM

MARINO MARINI

The Egyptian Museum of Florence was founded in the first decades of the 1800's with the objects of the Medici collection and with the acquisition by the Grand duke of Tuscany Leopold II of the collection of Giuseppe Nizzoli, diplomat of the Austrian consulate in Cairo (1824). Subsequently the same Grand duke, in 1828-29, promoted a French-Tuscan expedition in Egypt and Nubia guided by Ippolito Rossellini, the first true italian Egyptologist, and Jean Francois Champollion who first deciphered the hieroglyphic symbols. The double purpose of the expedition was that of seeking archaeological finds to enrich the Egyptian Museum, and to graphically reproduce the most important monuments of ancient Egypt. Later the Egyptian collection, enriched by the acquisition of the Ricci collection, was organized and displayed in the rooms of the ex-monastery of St. Catherine; and in 1853 it was transfered to via Faenza. In the following years the donations from private parties and the new acquired pieces with the expeditions in Egypt of Ernesto Schiapparelli made it absolutely necessary to transfer the museum to a new more spacious location; (in the meantime the Etruscan collections had been annexed to the others.) Therefore a palace was designated in 1879 as the new seat of the Archaeological Museum of Florence – the Palazzo della Crocetta in via della Colonna.

A little statue in limestone representing a servant who
grinds the wheat using two stone wheels appropriately
sharpened. Vth dynasty (c. 2400 B.C.) Room I cabinet 11.

Little statue in limestone of a maid who filters the 'barley loaves' to make beer, according to a procedure which is still in use in Egypt. Vth dynasty (c. 2400 B.C.) Room I cabinet 11.

▲
Funerary stele known as the "false door" for Kasut. Around the subject which represents the defunct there are formulae of offering of the donors of the stele. End of Ancient Kingdom (c. 2200 B.C.) Room I cabinet 12.

Headless statue of a pharaoh in rose granite. The ruler is shown sitting on the throne with his arms out-stretched on his thighs, according to the stylistic canons of the statuary of the XIIth dynasty (c. 1900 B.C.) Room I

In the vestibule in front of the stairs there are on display: a monolithic tabernacle in gray granite from the sanctuary of Iside on the island of File dedicated by Ptolemy VIII, Evergete II and Cleopatra III (dated from the middle of the 2nd century B.C.). There is also a sarcophagus in rose granite for the dignitary AMENEMHTSCNBE constructed under the commission of the sovereign SESOSTRI II of the XIIth dynasty (1897-1877 B.C.). It is one of the most beautiful sarcophaghi of the Middle Kingdom production.

On the first floor on the wall between the doors leading to the Egyptian collection and the collection of the small Etruscan urns there is a painting by G. Angelelli representing the members of the French-Tuscan expedition in Egypt (1828-29) with J.F. Champollion and I. Rossellini in the center.

Room I

– Statues in limestone of servants "servants of the tomb"; they are typical of the furnishings (funerary) of the Vth dynasty and were placed in the tomb so that they might procure the food that the defunct would need. Both statues have been heavily restored and some of the colors used in the past centuries render the reading rather difficult. (window cabinet 11)

– Stele in the form of a monumental façade for the singular ornament of the king KAUSUT; from the end of the Ancient Kingdom. In the central panel there is a female figure sitting in front of the offering table while holding a small vase for unguents in her left hand. All around there are inscriptions and formulations for the offering. This type of stele, called "the false door" was placed on one of the walls of the room of the sarcophagus and was to permit the spirit of the defunct to leave the tomb in order to take the offerings and then return again to his body. (cabinet 12)

– Stele for the instructor of the prophets, HOTPI; first intermediary period. On the left a couple is represented sitting in front of the table with the funerary offerings and in front of them is a male figure, standing, who holds a long cane and a sceptre; and there is a youth in reduced scale. (cabinet)...

Stele of Simentwoser. The defunct, holding a long staff, is represented sitting in front of the table of the funerary offerings. XIth dynasty. Room I cabinet 29.

Stele in the "false door" style for Khentekhtayaun. There are no figures, but there are transcribed the parental relationships of the relatives of the defunct. XIIth dynasty. Room I cabinet 35.

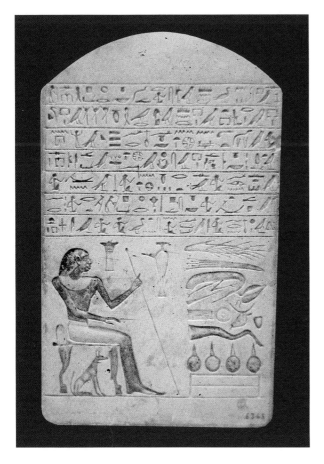

The significance of the egyptian stele is fundamentally funerary; it was in fact supposed to secure the funerary offerings and the prayers necessary for the defunct. It was inserted in a wall of the tomb and was offered by the relatives, servants and friends, as the incised texts and paintings reveal. Another meaning is that of the ex-voto. It was customary, for whomever went in pilgrimage to the famous temples, to offer a stele with their/his own image in the act of worshiping the divinity of that location. The stele, protected in the temple, at the moment of death of the offerers, then became the funerary stele and was therefore under the direct protection of the divinity. The other significance of the stele is a political one. With the stele the Pharaohs could exalt their military enterprises, their civil undertakings or projects and were represented either in the act of worshiping various divinities or standing in one of their war vehicles.

– Acephalous (headless) statue of a Pharaoh in rose granite, multilated right arm; XIIth dynasty. The statue was tampered with in a more recent period scraping away the original dedication and placing over it the dedication of PUMI in memory of his father SHESHONQ, prince of Busiris.

– Commemorative stele of SIMENTWOSER

XIth dynasty. Under the ritual inscriptions of offering the defunct is visible sitting on a stool with lion paw legs in the company of a little cat. On the offerings table there are situated various victuals, among those the head and heart of an ox. (cabinet 29)

– Stele for the superintendent of the prophets, INYOTEF, end XIth beginning XIIth dynasty. In the upper panel the defunct is sitting in front of the offerings table, on the other side his wife and his oldest son. Underneath the seven sons are represented on their knees. (cabinet 31)

– Stele for the major-domo KHENTEKHTAYAUN, XIIth dynasty. It is shaped in the form of a monumental façade and is an example of a genealogical table of a family, with even persons not of the same blood, but with particular ties to the family. (cabinet 35)

Room II

– Votive knives and Boomerangs in ivory with incised animal scenes which have the ritual purpose of propitiating the hunt, XIIth dynasty. (cabinet 6)

– Models of serving trolleys in wood; oars and boats in wood from the end of the XIth – beginning of the XIIth dynasty. These models of boats have a very precise religious significance: they were to transport the defunct to the kingdom of the dead in the presence of Osiris following the solar boat of the god Ra. They were placed in general in the private tombs; the Pharaohs instead, had real boats actually buried near their pyramids.

– Stele for the military campaign of SESOSTRI I (1971-1928 B.C.) XII th dynasty. In the left part the Pharaoh is represented with a low crown and two tall feathers while holding a long cane and a club. Two divinities flank him: the god Horus, in reduced scale behind him, and the warrior god Month who gives his benediction. Underneath them there is a line of prisoners each of which represents a city conquered during the victorius campaign in Nubia conducted by general Menthopte in the year XVIIIth of the reign of SESOSTRI I; the stele comes from the temple of Isis in Buhen.

– Stele for the functionary RENSONBE and his wife; end XII – beginning XIIIth dynasty. Above

there are two Ugiat eyes incised, the "eyes of Horus" which signify protection and security. In the niche the high relief of the married couple who hold hands. (cabinet 11)

– Stele for the scribe of the great prison, SIPTAH; XIIth dynasty. In the arched part there are two great Ugiat eyes. The defunct in the center of the stele is in the company of his wife and is sitting in front of the offerings table where he is paid homage by a kneeling couple. In the panel underneath, the twenty squatting figures represent the donors of the stele. (cabinet 15)

The materials on display in the other rooms are

Funerary covering painted for the mummy of the women Takerhed. The numerous painted figures represent the images of the protecting goddesses. Ptolemaic Epoch (304-30 B.C.) Room III.

momentarily closed for restoration.

Room III

– Acephalous statue in gray granite of THUTMOSI III; New Kingdom, XVIIIth dynasty. The Pharaoh is sitting on a throne and clasps to his chest the symbols of power (sceptre and whip) and under his feet there are represented nine arches which symbolize the enemies of Egypt.

– Statue in gray granite of PTAHMOSE, superintendent of treasury under the rule of AMENOPHIS III (1390-1352 B.C.) XVIIIth dynasty. The great priest is represented on his knees, typical position of an offerer.

– Funerary chests in painted wood from the "Low Epoch" and the Ptolemaic Epoch some of which still contain the mummy in a good state of conservation. Among these there is the mummy of the defunct

TEOS, son of Tromnubaste, of the Ptolemaic epoch.

According to the Egyptians, each living being was constituted of a number of parts: body, name, shadow, and two spiritual elements, KA and BA. While BA at the moment of death would fly into the sky in the presence of Osiris, the KA remained in the tomb next to the body of the defunct to protect him so that he would remain intact. Therefore the use of embalming and/or mummifying was most common to consent in a later period the reunification of the vital components and therefore the survival of the defunct in the other world. Originally, the mummifying was reserved only for the Pharaohs, direct representatives of Osiris; then it was also spread to the noble classes and later to those less elevated. The technique of embalming consisted, at first, in the exsiccation (drying) of the body which was done by heat or with the use of salts of a strong dehydrating nature. Then they removed

◄ **Portrait of a young woman on wood, of the type "El Fayum". Quite evident the strong influence of roman portraiture in the representation of the defunct. IInd century A.D. Room III**

Polychrome bas-relief with the goddess Hathor and the pharaoh Sethi I. The goddess, protectoress of women and one of the most venerated divinities of ancient Egypt, is represented with cow's horn and the solar disc. XIXth dynasty. Room II 2nd part.

the "soft" parts of the body (brain, liver, lungs, intestines) and after having carefully washed the cavaties, they filled them with bandages and resinous substances. When the process of exsiccation had terminated, the body was sprinkled with oils and unguents and lastly wrapped in intertwined linen bindings.

– Portrait of a young woman on wood; IIcentury B.C. This small tablet is called "El-Fayum type" (the place where many portraits of this type come from) and it was placed on the face of the mummy.

– Box in wood for Canopic vases, XIXth dynasty. The chest was used to contain four Canopic vases and is decorated with the figures of the protective divinities. The Canopi are particular vases that were to conserve the soft parts of the defunct removed before the body was mummified. The cover of each of these represents a protective divinity of one of the parts of the body: Amset with a human head, for the liver; Hapi, baboon, for the lungs; Duamutef, jackal, for the stomach; Kebehsenuf, hawk, for the intestines.

– Two-faced statue of Bes; Ptolemaic Epoch. It represents the god Bes (protecting demon of women, children and the family); the two-facedness of Bes was for the purpose of spreading his protective power in more than one direction, while his terrifying appearance served to frighten away evil spirits.

– Chip of limestone with sketched designs of heads of sovereigns, among which one is outstanding for the refined finishing and the intensity of colors; XIXth dynasty.

– Sarcophagus in painted wood of TJESREPERET, wet-nurse of the daughter of the Ethiopian Pharaoh Taharqa, XXVth dynasty. The sarcophagus comes from the tomb of the necropolis of Sheikh Abd El-Qurna, found in 1829 by Rossellini intact. Other objects from the same tomb are displayed in the egyptian rooms of the museum, as for example the beautiful specimen of a mirror in gilded bronze with its cover in wood – perfectly conserved. (Room VIII)

Room II (2nd part)

– Stele for the priest of Ptah, PTAHMOSE; from

◄ Bas-relief of the goddess Maat, from the tomb of the pharaoh Sethi I. The ostrich feather is her personal symbol and signifies "justice", truth. XIXth dynasty. Room II 2nd part.

At the following page.
Pieces of bas-relief with the official Ptahmose receiving the gifts lovingly offered by the children. XIXth dynasty. Room II 2nd part.

Fragment of a bas-relief with the functionary Ptahmose waiting to receive the gifts that his sons affectionately offer him. XIXth dynasty (1293-1190 B.C.) Room II 2nd part.

Saqqara, mid-XVIIIth dynasty. It is a stele in a pyramid form and presents, above, a niche with a male figure in high relief. Lower down, there is a man sitting and holding two types of sceptres; in front of him another male figure is standing and is pouring a liquid over a support. On the external sides of the stele the wife of the deceased and his sister are represented.

– Fragment of a wall relief from Saqqara; XXVIth dynasty. There are represented, in two registers, various artisans at work. From the left, above, one recognizes potters and sculptors, blacksmiths working with metals; in the register

below there are two engravers of hard stones, shoemakers and wagon constructors.

– From the tomb of Sethi I (1291-1279 B.C.) discovered in 1817 by G.B. Belzoni in the Valley of the Kings at Thebes: a relief in polychrome in which a Pharaoh is represented with a wig and a long transparent tunic while he receives as a gift a precious necklace from the goddess Hathor, with cow's horn and a solar disc on her head. The goddess Hathor was one of the most important egyptian divinities and was the protectoress of women, goddess of love, fecundity and of pleasure. Also, a bas-relief in polychrome where one sees the

goddess Maat with an ostrich feather, symbol to identify her. In the inscription the goddess is recognized as "daughter of Ra, lady and patron of the necropolis". She was also venerated as the goddess of truth and justice. Both reliefs are datable from the XIXth dynasty.

– Bas-relief of the scribes, necropolis of Thebes, XVIIIth dynasty. Four scribes are very ably incised with tablets and styluses, in the position of he who writes from dictation.

– Fragment of a bas-relief in polychrome from the tomb of Ptahmose at Memphis, XIXth dynasty. The high functionary, sitting in the company of his wife (whom we can barely see), receives funerary offerings from his numerous sons.

– Funerary stele of the Late Epoch of the canon of the orating priests of Osiris in Abydos, Penbu. In the roundish pediment or fronton there is the solar disc (Horo) with wide-spread wings. In the center of the stele the defunct is with his hands raised in sign of his devotion; first he is in the act of adoration to Horo (with the head of a hawk and solar disc) and then to Aton ("the sun which sets" with the crowns of the Kingdoms of High and Low Egypt). Both these divinities have long sceptres and the sign of Aneh (=life). The object which we partially see behind the arms of the deceased is the instrument used by the orating priests to determine the calculation of night hours with the observation of the stars.

– Statue of the goddess Hathor with the resemblance of a cow, and the Pharaoh Horemheb; XVIIIth dynasty. The Pharaoh is nursed by the goddess; milk, in fact, in ancient Egypt, was considered a means of purification and resurrection. With Horemheb (1319-1293 B.C.) they turned back to the cult of Amon (god of the city of Thebes) after his predecessor, Amenophis IV (Akhenaton; 1352-1336 B.C.) had attempted a religious reformation with the institution of the monotheistic cult of Aton, the solar disc.

– Stone sarcophagus belonging to the dignitary Bakenrenef; XXVIth dynasty. The sarcophagus is entirely decorated with divinities, magic symbols and ritual inscriptions. On the cover the goddess Nut is represented with open arms in the act of protecting the defunct.

– Stele for the Vizier Dhutmose, middle of the XVIIIth dynasty. In the form of a monumental façade, it presents a long series of inscriptions and in the central panel the defunct appears sitting with his arm out-stretched towards the offering table. The man standing in front of him is his son, who had dedicated the stele.

– Stele of Tekha'e, woman musician of Amon; XIX dynasty. It is typical of the area of Thebes because of its triangular pediment which represents the little pyramids constructed above the Thebes tombs. In the fronton there is the god Anubi (jackal) while in the two registers underneath the defunct is in the act of worshiping Osiris; and the goddess Hathor is pouring purified water on the hands of the woman.

Room VI

– Little statues of "Usciabti". These statuettes had the ritual function of substituting the defunct in the work(s) which the defunct could be called to do in the other world by Osiris, the lord of the 'beyond the tomb'. "Usciabti" means, in fact, "he who responds" and it was actually their duty to respond if the defunct was called upon to carry on some activities. They are represented as little mummies usually in stone or faience with their hands crossed on their breast and which hold the working tools (hoe, scythe, etc...). On each one the magic formula is written which serves to animate them.

Room VII

– Mummies of animals (cats, dogs, serpents, fish and birds) with their respective X-rays. The technique for the mummification is the same used for human beings. The practice of embalming animals is found above all in the last period of the egyptian civilisation when the true significance of the religion was nearly lost and the animal, (by burying its remains) which had been a living symbol of the divinity, becomes instead the means by which one could be in grace with the divinity itself. In a number of locations there existed "cemeteries" for animals, often specific according to the local cult,

Chalice in glazed terracotta (faience) in the shape of a
lotus flower. This type of ceramic was used to imitate the
precious vases of gold and silver of the princes and
pharaohs. XVIIIth dynasty. Room VIII

where thousands of animal mummies were grouped in underground rooms most of which contained in amphorae.

– Bust of a woman in limestone; end of the XVIIIth dynasty. Perhaps it was part of a sitting statue. Most intersting is the wig, so-called "enveloping", characteristic of the kingdom of Amenophis III. In her left hand she holds a lotus flower.

– Statue of Henat; XXVIth dynasty, reign of Amasi (570-526 B.C.) The priest is standing and is clean shaven/bald as was required in his religious position. With his hands he supports a stele on which are listed all the positions he held in the city of Sais.

– Bust of a dignitary, XXVIIth dynasty. He wears a head dress typical of the Saitica Epoch, the Khat, and a persian type necklace.

– Statue of Ptahmose; XVIIIth dynasty, reign of Amenophis III. It represents the great priest of the god Ptah, protector of artists, crouching with his legs on his knees.

Room VIII

– Vases in terracotta, objects in straw and wood, objects for the toilette including a mirror in gilded bronze from the tomb of Tjesreperet, wet-nurse of the daughter of the Pharaoh Taharqa.

– War cart, XVIIIth dynasty, from Thebes. It was made with various types of wood and some of the parts of the bindings have been restored. The war cart or wagon and the horse were first introduced in Egypt by an invading people, Hyksos, during the Middle Kingdom; and just these innovations rendered the egyptian army invicible from the XVIIIth dynasty until the Late Kingdom.

– Chalice in glazed terracotta in the shape of a lotus flower; XVIIIth dynasty. This kind of ceramic, called faience, assumes a particular importance during the New Kingodm and has as its predominating colors green and azure. The chalices in the shape of a lotus flower belong in this classification with the petals rendered in relief or else painted.

– Stele in painted wood of the woman

Tentpessumedju of the Late Epoch. The pediment is surmounted by a wooden statuette symbolizing the spirit-bird (Ba) with the solar disc on the head. In the first register there is the boat of the solar god Ra (with the head of a ram) with whom he traveled in the sky. The bird on the right represents the Ba (spirit of the deceased). In the second register the defunct appears in the act of worshiping four squatting divinities: Osiris, Isis, Neftis and Horo.

Chronological Table with the names of the most important pharaohs and the principal events of each period.

PRE-DYNASTIC PERIOD (5000-3100 B.C.)
Thinita Age
I dynasty (3100-2890 B.C.)
Menes
Unification of High and Low Egypt
Writing appears.
II dynasty (2890-2686 B.C.)
Funerary architecture develops.

Ancient Kingdom
III dynasty (2686-2613 B.C.)
Zoser
IV dynasty (2613-2494 B.C.(
Cheope – Chefren – Micerino
The great pyramids of Giza are constructed.
Military campaigns in Nubia.
V dynasty (2494-2345 B.C.)
VI dynasty (2345-2181 B.C.)
The drafting of the first religious texts. Construction of princes' tombs.

First Intermediary Period
VII-X dynasty (2181-2133 B.C.)
The unity of the Kingdom is lost and each province acquires its own autonomy.

Middle Kingdom
XI dynasty (2133-1991 B.C.)
Menthotpe I and III
The princes of Thebes bring back up the central power.
XII dynasty (1991-1786 B.C.)
Sesostri I and III – Amenemhet I and III
Victorious campaigns in Nubia.

Second Intermediary Period
XIII-XVII dynasty (1786-1570 B.C.)
Invasion of the Hyksos who conquer the north of the country.
New Kingdom
XVIII dynasty (1570-1293 B.C.)
Thutmosi I and III – Amenofi III – Amenofi IV (Akhenaton) – Tutankhamon – Horemheb

The invading people are driven out. Artistic rebirth and numerous political and religious reforms.
XIX dynasty (1293-1190 B.C.)
Ramesse I and II – Sethi I – Mernptah
The maximum expansion of Egypt.
XX dynasty (1190-1070 B.C.)
Ramesse III
Late Kingdom
XXI-XXXI dynastry (1070-332 B.C.)
Priests rise to power and the various invasions of foreign
peoples bring about the fall of the central power. Only
during the XXVIth dynasty (Psammetico I, Amasi) there is a
brief period of autonmy but in 525 B.C. the persian invasion
definitively cancels the dreams of rebirth of the egyptian
kingdom.

Macedonian Conquest (332-304 B.C.)
Alexander the Great

Ptolemaic Epoch (304-30 B.C.)
The successors of Alexander the Macedonian choose Alexandria
as capital which will become one of the most important cities
of the Mediterranean in the Hellenistic Age.

Annexation to the Roman Empire
In 30 B.C. after the suicide of Cleopatra.

Silver Amphora (Baratti) IV Century after Christ ▶